A BOOK OF CINQUAINS
REVISED EDITION

A BOOK OF CINQUAINS

REVISED EDITION

Andrew Mangravite
Illustrations by Carolee Karpell

Copyright © 2014 by Andrew Mangravite.
Illustrations copyright 2014 by Carolee Karpell.

Library of Congress Control Number: 2014905424
ISBN: Hardcover 978-1-4931-8798-0
Softcover 978-1-4931-8797-3
eBook 978-1-4931-8799-7

All rights reserved. No part of this book may be reproduced or transmitted in any form or by any means, electronic or mechanical, including photocopying, recording, or by any information storage and retrieval system, without permission in writing from the copyright owner.

This book was printed in the United States of America.

Rev. date: 05/08/2014

To order additional copies of this book, contact:
Xlibris LLC
1-888-795-4274
www.Xlibris.com
Orders@Xlibris.com

Curtain

rung down; flutter

of a lady fanning,

that quickly in the empty streets

it's night.

A sea,

her unbound hair

will wash the iris so

tenderly, sailors might cherish

that shore.

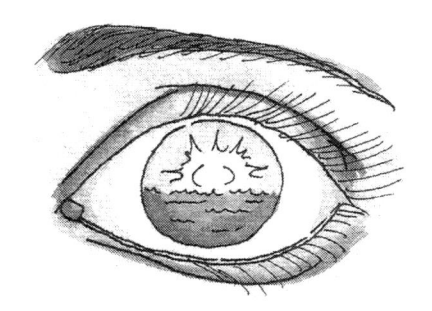

The breeze

in gentle waves

harmonized these things:

the odors of the soil, the cries

of birds.

04/18/76.

Sometimes

a passing breeze

will outline the body

to make one's brain become aware:

I am.

07/31/76.

Cut roses,

petals and leaves,

delicate tissue all,

but in their color and shape, exact,

gem-like.

08/22/76.

Raining;

I recall her

jumping over puddles;

she was barefooted, I always

wore shoes.

08/26/76.

To die,

must be a leaf

falling into blackness

of stream, or swirling in a wind

so high . . . .

10/22/76.

Summer

comes to meadows

all the green things groan in

pained erection; insects shriek

colors.

10/30/76.

Sure foot

autumn winds stalk

through streets and empty parks

even lovers have fled these places—

fair game.

12/28/76.

Palm tree

fronds rustle breezes,

women with long fingers

lost in admiration, reaching

to touch.

Sunset

incarnadines

barren winter forests;

O let the coldness in my heart

now melt.

Snapping,

the brittle ice

of the cicada's cry

gone, now this summer night begins

to thaw.

Hungry

November's winds

cry out to eat the earth,

a poor fare: dusty fields, bare trees,

and stones.

She is

of the river,

and loves of many men

have been but diverse streams running

through her.

Phantom!

your pale skin's myth

once haunted Bellocq's nights,

upon your divan you became

his soul.

Beauty

chastens the man

who would pursue it, as

icy fields burn the tramping feet

of fools.

01/20/78.

Snow falls

indifferent

and lies on the earth an

openly hostile, beautiful

hatred.

01/23/78.

Landscapes

of my childhood

fall away, tree by tree

hill by hill, my slate's washed clean

by rain.

08/10/78.

By rain

earth becomes mud

and that mud is turned

to thick brown water flowing on

in time.

08/10/78.

Flirting

jellyfish dart

in and out of shadows . . .

braced against wind, a seagull

screams love.

11/23/95.

Panting,

old dog plunges

into the water, swims and swims—

suddenly youthful and graceful,

and free . . . .

11/23/95.   "Fetching."

God's tops

spin on for years

before they wobble—then,

"Master, come and fix this life that's

broken!"

12/07/95.   "Feast of St. Ambrose."

Lately,

I have seen ducks

that seemed to tarry,

human like, too long where pleasure's

fleeting.

12/22/95.   "The Procrastinators."

I go

quiet, alone,

wrapped in this coldness

which never fails to cradle me . . .

a womb.

01/01/97.   "Walking. New Year's Day."

Insults

to marble sky,

winged cemeteries

singing their dirges to themselves—

two crows!

01/02/97.   "Borrowed Feathers."

Softly

and everywhere

these myriad pin pricks

raise up a rustled protest from

sere leaves.

01/05/97.   "Warm Winter Rain."

So deep

a blue-gray sky

turns seagulls into fish;

so bright a sun makes even crows

glassy.

01/07/97. "Intense."

Grandly

big wind shakes trees

like helpless children lost,

jeers at the hapless orphans of

the fall.

01/08/97. "Melodramatic."

Sowing

their harshest cries

in fleecy white furrows

these somber farmers hope for rich

harvests.

01/12/97.   "And their crops are the fruits of discord . . ."

Not so

that wind tears down—

it challenges all things,

wraps itself 'round them and defines

their form.

01/16/97.   "Sculptor."

Creeping

cold leeches life

making springy twig-tips

stiff and unyielding—touch them and

they snap.

01/19/97.   "Brittle."

Today

is such a day

as never was because

your eyes met mine, smiling at me

today.

01/27/97.   "Love Song."

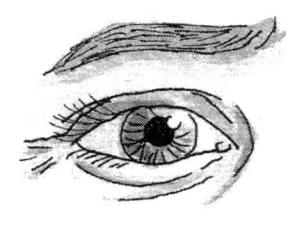

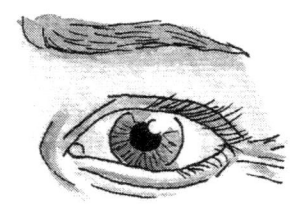

Just now—

warm coat undone

colder air rushes in,

spreading out against my chest so

quickly.

01/31/97.

Typing—

words follow words,

thoughts come and go away—

what ought to go, what ought to stay

today?

02/02/97.   "Revisions."

Night air

more fragrant than

the bright, warm air of day

gives to nostrils what it withholds

from eyes.

02/07/97. "Compensation."

What's this—

bright snow's blanket,

all rumpled and torn,

is being kicked aside now—

by seeds!

02/09/97. "Rent."

Gently

sleep conquers us

but irresistibly,

stronger than steel bands; who resists

these yawns?

02/10/97.   "Sleepy."

Relax,

even while earth

awaits your rapid fall . . .

do not resist its stiff embrace,

go soft.

02/12/97.   "Advice on Falling."

Puppy,

eager to share

hungry for approval

flops over on its head—silly

lover.

02/23/97.   "Faux-pas."

Hotel,

small but noisy—

this bush where sparrows roost,

invisible tenants who are

not shy!

02/24/97.   "Avian Dive."

No words

once said can be

unsaid, so it happens

that anger's tell hangs in the air

like smoke.

02/25/97.   "Fine Haze."

Something

lives in this air

fearsome and sad—a mass

of disappointments and bad dreams,

stale air.

02/27/97.   "Old House."

Wishing

is my pleasure,

not hope which can mislead;

one can wish for the moon, one hopes

for earth.

02/28/97. "Limits."

Erect

as fine troopers

and bold with inbred hope,

these crocuses proclaim their faith

in Spring.

03/02/97. "A Day for Mr. Starbuck."

Because

it's just one flake

I question if it's real

or some trick of my mind, or else

a speck.

03/03/97.   "Pathfinder."

Firstling,

I have seen you—

delicate yellow cup

trusting as child and hopeful as

parent.

03/08/97.   "Flower."

How strange!

seeing a glove

crawling on the pavement,

filled with human essence, going

nowhere.

03/09/97. "Lost."

Dripping

from every branch

not sweet sleep of poets,

but cold, wet snow fast melting in

sun's light.

03/10/97. "Thaw."

Funny!

well, maybe cute . . .

you trees look like children

with reddish burrs, but soon those leaves

age you.

03/11/97.   "Potential."

Always

there is the need

to accomplish the goal,

to force the words that will create

this thing.

03/13/97.   "Drive."

Today

we honor you

Joseph, patron and guide,

humble man who fled from kings, who

held God.

03/19/97.   "Feast of St. Joseph."

Comet,

my search for you

was no success—neither

head nor tail would your modesty

disclose.

03/23/97.   "Bopping."

Money

can't abide me;

it gives itself rarely,

can hardly wait to leave my hands

empty.

04/04/97.   "The Fleering Fleece."

A leaf

spiraling down

becomes an absent wall

for the work-in-progress nest of

a crow.

04/06/97.   "Home Improvement."

A cloud

gave way, and then—

for only an instant—

this too-gray street was gilded by

sunlight.

04/07/97.   "In Passing."

Because

the falling rain

comes from the sky we find

our cherish'd insularity

fails us.

04/12/97.   "On Earth In Rain."

Dinner,

fat and juicy

on a concrete platter . . .

fit for cardinal's palate, this

earthworm.

04/13/97.   "Meat On the Table!"

Tiny

and so noisy

perfect simulacrum of

mindless aggression set loose in

a tree.

04/15/97.   "Woodpecker."

Hazy,

a pearl set on

a cotton pad, the sun

is trying to shine joy but it's

so hard!

04/17/97.   "Gray and Lumpen Day."

Breathing

asthmatic'ly

wind batters walls,

shakes trees, makes a mess of things,

suffers.

04/19/97.   "Wheez."

Look there!

four fat robins,

each in its position . . .

they seem about to dance, but wait

to eat.

04/26/97.   "Hunter's Ball."

Strains of

Albinoni

are not much help on days

when misfortunes fall like peals of

Mahler.

04/28/97.   "Music Appreciation Lesson."

Behind

a window blind

a spider's on the prowl

and in the moted sunlight flies

will die.

04/30/97. "Sneaky Death."

Topsoil

moist and clumped

gritty yet yielding dream

of future abundance tall

and green.

05/05/97. "Hope in Hand."

Gulping

the hapless worm

greedy robin apes death,

swallows life whole, without pause to

savor.

05/10/97.   "Dining Out."

Swiftly

robin lets fly

a white streak of bird shit;

it is quite beautiful in its

elan.

05/13/97.   "The Toilet."

Spider

perambulates

blithely unconcerned

that this floor is wide and far from

shelter.

05/14/97. "Providence Illumined."

Truly

Master Crow is

a giant among birds

when he passes, mere sparrows are

awe struck.

05/18/97. "He's an eagle! He's a pterosaur!"

Starling's

black pants are tight—

what an ungainly gait—

but his Chinese lacquer coat is

"tres chic!"

05/19/97.   "Fashion Plate."

Pity

the poor earthworm—

a yeoman in the soil,

in water, dead, and in the air,

a meal.

05/20/97.   "And fire will burn it . . ."

Forward

motion funnels

a sea of frantic legs;

we are racing along paths of

habit.

05/21/97.   "The Flow."

Irked

by my presence

squirrel jumps from branch to branch

pauses to check me out—still there,

the pest!

05/26/97.   "Space Invader."

Clipping

their spiky shoots

these bushes remind me

how much they are like men: stubborn

and harsh.

05/27/97.   "Family."

end of the first part of

A Book of Cinquains

Squirrel

sitting upright

an anxious waiter

surveying an empty lawn—your

order?

06/04/97. "Attentive."

Too cold

for many bugs—

this springtime seems empty

without bustling of armored

lordlings.

06/05/97. "Absent"

"Again"—

a tricky word

suggesting a new chance;

but will mere repetition be

the charm?

06/08/97.   "A Regret."

A hug

from Mother Earth,

heat rises to greet me,

I dwell in her embrace and know

her love.

06/10/97.   "Dry Heat."

Descents—

Holy Spirit,

Crown-of-Thorns—perhaps

this hints to us true sanctity

will hurt.

06/13/97.   "Emblematic."

Starlings

never at rest

from patrolling the earth

hop and peck; move on; hop and peck;

move on.

06/15/97.   "The Active Life."

Earthworm

leads with its face—

a stupid thing to do!—

no wonder it can't see robins

for dirt.

06/16/97.   "Tunnel-Vision."

Glassy

and everywhere

underfoot, bits of slag

shine in sunlight, so beautiful

yet waste . . . .

06/17/97.   "Hopewell."

Hola!

Old pigeon

you'll have to do better—

the step isn't that high—it's hard

to die.

06/19/97.　　　　　"Getting Ready."

One wing

hangs in a web

turning delicately

when sunlight strikes it, it shines, a

jewel.

06/24/97.　　　　　"The Remains."

Ghostly

this dot of light

floating down the hallway

on a summer night—a lonely

firefly.

06/25/97.   "The Searching Light."

Squeezing

past my eyesight

the neighbor's cat en route

to mid-morning adventures

glides by.

06/27/97.   "Not So Fast!"

How odd!

Inside a box—

with its cover on it—

I've found a dead cockroach somehow

trapped.

07/01/97. "Surprise!"

Quiet,

velvet blackness,

fabric of humid air—

relentless rain leaves it all in

tatters.

07/03/97. "Midnight Caller."

Tumult!

Caught in the lurch

rash squirrel can not go

anywhere without meeting a

sharp beak . . . .

07/06/97.   "Squirrel and Mocking Birds."

Pretty

purple flower

peeking from our holly—

who would believe such beauty is

a weed?

07/09/97.   "Appearances."

Down there

you see a man

leaning against a pole

on a street corner in Yeadon

waiting.

07/10/97.   "Self-Portrait as Satellite Photo."

Leaping

into the air

starling takes leave of us

scandalized at being caught

off-guard.

07/14/97.   "The Secret Revealed."

Rubies

of my delight—

two plum tomatoes glow

like lamps in a shadowy green

tangle.

07/20/97.   "Ripe."

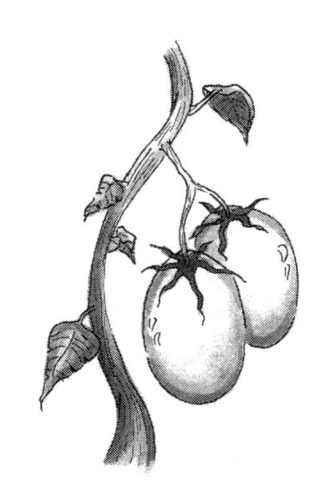

Writing

so hurriedly—

no way to do poems;

cinquains should be meditations

not burps.

07/21/97.

Raining

sometimes in Spain

and sometimes in Yeadon;

saving lives here, taking them there—

just rain.

07/24/97.

Unknown

to all the rest,

the subtle stone resides

where there's no shortage of base lead

to turn.

07/26/97.

Darkens

and grows cooler . . .

then there's this hush, breaths held

we are all waiting for the rain

to fall.

07/27/97.   "Yes . . . ?"

Robin

strikes a fine pose—

impassive, heroic—

but his toothpick legs betray his

weak knees.

07/31/97.   "Poseur."

Too late

for digger wasps,

cicada's snow-white gut

is being mined for its riches

by ants.

08/03/97.   "Fast Work."

How proud

starling's cousin

the mockingbird can be—

no fancy duds but, my, his tail's

held high.

08/05/97.   "Poor, but Proud."

Horse feeds

untroubled by

this great blue dragonfly

a needle sewing sheets of heat

in place.

08/11/97.

Merchant

with bulging stores,

spider has a nice spot

in a corner where lots of flies

blunder.

08/14/97.   "Location. Location. Location."

Great are

paintings, movies

and all the myths of men

whereby we entertain ourselves

'til death.

08/16/97.

An ant

blown from my hand

falls from a skyscraper

in human terms, but hits the ground and

runs off.

08/17/97.   "It's only an ant."

Raining . . .

air sticks to skin

and bad smells hang in air

endlessly . . . a nice sort of life

for fish!

08/18/97.   "Murk."

So much

rain has fallen,

everything is hiding

beneath water-logged shelters

of woe.

08/20/06.   "In my heart too, Paul."

Often

the trees resound

with cicadas' singing

'til silence dropping like a shade

startles.

08/26/97.

Token

of fond farewell

a single feather peeks

from a bush where perhaps there was

a nest.

08/27/97.   "Rent."

Humid

air turns fragrant

a sixty-year old door

sanded, yields up its essence, sweet

cedar.

09/02/97.

Killing

as it came on

cold overtook them choking

their songs—and the cicadas fell

like leaves.

09/03/97. "Silent Morning."

Hopeful,

a cricket waits

by a closed window,

"Open and let me in—winter's

coming."

09/08/97.   "Timing Is Everything."

Stranger

than a stranger

at a back room confab

where goodies are apportioned—

my life.

09/09/97.

"In sheets"—

people say that

about the way rain falls,

but it's really more like glass rods

pounding.

09/11/97.   "Pistons."

Notice

"humble" sparrow's

beady black eyes glinting—

think he's happy about being small? He

could spit!

09/12/97.   "Diary of a Cowardly Impudent."

Darting

hither and yon

indecision's model,

squirrel seems frantic with choices

to make.

09/14/97.   "In Circles."

Fewer

to see each day,

the insects and the birds

are packing up to leave us, say

good-bye.

09/22/97.   "Show's Over."

Squirrels'

busy season

is here—each one you see

has a nut in its mouth or hands—

rushing . . . .

09/23/97.   "Margin Call."

He's gone.

The Saint has left—

flowers, insects and birds

soon will follow him, leaving us

the worse.

10/03/97.   "Transitus."

Mild day—

sun feels so warm,

flowers take courage and

perk themselves up—winter's still far

away.

10/04/97.   "On the Feast of St. Francis."

Majos

knives in their capes,

the two bandy fellows

hop about . . . each trying to be

higher . . . .

10/07/97.   "Dueling Mockingbirds."

We go

trotting gaily

from faux-pas to faux-pas—

war, rapine, corruption—who will

blame us?

10/08/97.   "Merry Wanderers."

Big toys

caught in sunlight

freeze like statues—

afraid to buzz, whistle or turn

cartwheels.

10/11/97.   "At Storm King Park."

Cotton

wads of sky choke

morning's ambitions—

what's there to do on such a day,

but dream?

10/13/97.

Pissy

and pseudo-rain,

you make clean air feel like

sloppy, wet kisses blown at me

by life.

10/15/97.

From rain

to sunlight—all

in the space of a day—

change rules all though all proceeds from

changeless.

10/18/97.

Ignore

that pigeon—

it can hardly help you

to find nutritious nuts, besides

it's dead.

10/24/97.   "The Levite Squirrel."

Time drips

through day's faucet,

and day dissolves itself

in gray clouds and fine rain until

I yawn . . . .

10/25/97.   "Dissolution."

Two crows

making music

each sings a different song

loudly and with authority—

like men!

10/26/97.   "The Choristers."

Cracking

a wide, wide smile

noon shakes off morning's gloom

relieves us of the burden of

our cares.

10/27/97. "Come Out and Play."

Follow

all the right signs,

come out at the wrong door!

Sometimes one misconception damns

a life.

10/28/97.

Tumbling

through empty air,

exploding the silence,

the notes protest repetition . . .

in vain!

10/31/97.   "Tuning."

Like birds

hopping on lawns

dead leaves tumble along,

slyly mimicking life—pets of

Autumn.

11/06/97.   "Mimics."

Weary

as Croesus

but hungry for one more,

squirrel holds his acorn tightly,

searches . . . .

11/07/97.

Damp cold

is upon us

and my neighbor's flowers

refuse to surrender, flaunt their

colors.

11/13/97.

Like blood

oozing from wounds

the Japanese maple

has let go its leaves grudgingly,

in pain . . . .

11/14/97.

Watched

the pot never

boils, so the old saw says—

but when it's neglected, it never

simmers!

11/16/97.   "See-Saw."

Squirrel

psalmodizes:

"Praise be handy boughs,

and big meaty nuts—damnation

to cats!"

11/18/97.

Feeding

without ado,

this crow big as a hen

celebrates its utter crow-ness,

strutting.

11/21/97.   "Feeling Good."

Cricket

lies on its back

eyes full of sky, and arms

all neatly joined in endless

prayer.

11/22/97.   "Prayer of the Dead."

Sharing

one narrow roof,

squirrel and crow searching

for tasty morsels, but finding

nothing.

11/23/97.

No fun

being a leaf

caught up in a strong wind

whirled higher and higher, then

dropped.

11/24/97.   "A Plaything of the Heartless Gods."

Reindeer . . .

long horns, sharp hooves . . .

hardly playful-looking,

they'll kill you without thinking twice,

Santa.

11/29/97.   "The Real Rudolph."

He saw

You first, but then

another took his place.

Let us honor Andrew, selfless

lover.

11/30/97.   "Feast of St. Andrew."

So cold—

squirrels gallop,

crows rule the sky, sparrows

hide beneath the bushes . . . Winter

holds sway.

12/01/97.

Scatter

of pale green leaves

still spangles bare boughs

in this season of endings, grim

Winter.

12/04/97.

Seeping

into the bones

this wretched cold transforms

your supple flesh into a husk

that cracks.

12/06/97.   "Wind Chill."

Gently

setting each foot

(best one forward!) duck strolls

pondside, shakes a sprightly ass and

wades in.

12/09/97.   "On the Jersey Riviera."

Squawking

from concealment

squirrel berates the day:

"Would that the sun were shining and

I, young!"

12/11/97.   "Old Squirrel's Plaint."

Dying's

no easier than

living—a lucky few

slip and fall into a dream that's

endless.

12/12/97.   "Dream-Time."

Sometimes

cutting cookies

isn't so cut-and-dried;

dough will stick and tear—it's messy

like life.

12/13/97.

Must be

lovely for leaves

to be at the center

where power never shifts though winds

do blow.

12/14/97.   "On Observing a Pile of Leaves."

Flutter

in the bushes,

frantic moving shadows . . .

and from out the underbrush come

sparrows.

12/18/97.   "Big Deal!"

Here's where

the crows hold court

flapping in the high trees,

handing down their verdicts on life's

mishaps.

12/20/97.   "In the Bare Woods."

Wind-blown

oak seeds planted

in this cement garage

never grow tall, or become oak trees

at all.

12/25/97.   "Arrested."

First snow

falling all day

outstayed it's welcome,

we made rude sounds but it ignored

our fleers.

12/27/97.   "Go Away!"

Etched

in last night's snow,

brutal as a mirror,

every crooked branch's ways are

made straight.

12/28/97.   "Revelation."

Riding

past a river

whose waters are flowing

in the opposite direction . . .

my life.

12/29/97.   "Correspondence."

Year's done

for you, squirrel!

Big furry lima bean,

food for crows, were all those hoarded nuts

worth it?

12/31/97.   "God Visits the Rich Squirrel in a Dream."

end of the second part of

A Book of Cinquains

Muskrats

in death never

seem to find sweet repose;

their teeth are bared, like angry

losers.

01/30/99.   "Endtime."

Startled

by your whiteness

you, pristine page, amaze;

not with mere possibilities

you glow . . . .

01/31/99.

Andy

on his treadmill

feels like Crawly—though

Crawly seems to take more pleasure

from it.

02/03/99. "Portrait of the Artist as
a Hampster."

Monarch

of all he sees,

starling mounts his grand throne—

the trash dumpster holding all his

riches.

02/05/99. "To the Victor . . ."

Goodbyes

leave you cold;

in February's chill,

there nothing left to warm your

heart's hearth.

02/22/99.

Playing

tall trees like harps

the sure fingered wind

serenades us until our teeth

chatter.

03/04/99.   "Applause."

Courting

two squirrels dance

a jitterbug across

swaying branches; lust blinds us to

danger.

03/06/99. "Entranced."

Nice day.

I'm unhappy

but for no one reason . . .

a bag caught in our tree's like me—

empty.

03/16/99.

Sky boy,

through raw, gone voids

your diamond vision drives

a thousand sorry rains of death

to me.

1/31-2/25/99.   (for N.S.)

Grayness

solemn, bowed

life turned in upon

endless contemplation of its

ruin.

(12/28/94.)   "A Sunflower in December."

I ache,

feeling alone,

yet I ignore the ache—

far greater than my own—of Christ,

disown'd.

04/02/99.   "Good Friday."

Rainy,

cold—a foul day—

pigeons look all in,

strolling like shoppers with no

money.

04/11/99.   "Low Sunday."

Paint chips

tell the whole tale—

"white" is not absolute

like Truth, rather there are sixteen

shadings!

04/14/99.   "Milkpod or Coconut?"

Today

was pebble's day—

so small and smooth it held

me captivated by its pure

self-love.

04/24/99.

Inside

an apartment

gutted and forgotten

a gray suit hangs limp, waiting for

its ghost.

04/30/99.

Perched

atop the cross

atop our church, the crow

assumes a vatic mien but then

says naught.

05/12/99.   "Evermore."

Starling,

grown old and ill,

waits in the street for you,

kind car, to come and take it far

away.

05/18/99.   "An Avian Suicide."

Robin

and mockingbird,

sharing a confidence,

walk like diplomats posing for

pictures.

06/01/99.   "Photo-Op."

In Hell

I am certain

there are no winds to blow;

no, everything is still and close—

a dream . . . .

06/07/99.   "The Weather in Hell."

The snake

considered

as an animal fails—

it has no legs, no sense of style,

eats dirt.

06/08/99.

Ticking

grandfather clock

speaks in the voices of

the dear departed ones whose shades

reign here.

06/12/99.   "Visiting."

Dreary,

dreary day, you

seep right into my bones

you rain and rain for me 'til I

dissolve.

06/21/99.

Grasping

a six-inch twig

in its beak, the pigeon

pauses to dream of statelier

mansions.

06/27/99.   "Dream House."

Stairway

eaten by rust

just hangs over waters

rushing swiftly by—ornament

of time.

(06/06/99.)   "Near Sputin Duyvil Station."

Walking

I looked up

full of knowledge,

and saw a squirrel staring back

at me.

07/07/99.

Heartbeat

of the summer,

cicada cries govern

the passage of hours, unsettling

our dreams.

07/16/99.

Trouble

like a heat wave

ends in a thunderstorm

and always hangs around your town

too long.

07/26/99.

The wasps

stage their dogfights

with lazy precision—

there's game afoot but it's too hot

to hunt.

07/28/99.

Nature's

own "femme fatale"

the Japanese beetle

expects its beauty will excuse

its harm.

07/31/99.   "All in green . . ."

Untold

happiness waits

just over the next hill—

the one that towers to a height

untold.

08/03/99.

Playing

tag on the lawn

robins run circles 'round

last night's lottery ticket, a

dead play.

08/06/99.   "Things With Feathers."

Pecking,

hopping, hopping,

pecking—sparrows wander

barren lawns, a tribe in search of

manna.

08/10/99.   "Trust Me."

Folly

invites me in

for a home-cooked meal

of ashes—does she take me for

a corpse?

08/11/99.

Trying

to outrun rain,

I'm wet anyway, but

sweat isn't rain, my victory

is small.

08/14/99.

Meadows,

black and rolling,

far as the eye can see,

ready to sprout a bumper crop

of rain.

08/22/99.

Sunlight's

in retreat now—

just one patch on the floor

reminds the eyes of noontime's past

glories.

08/23/99.

Funny

Charlie Chaplin

kicks people in the ass

then jumps right over them, just like

real life.

08/28/99.

Winding

down quickly now

this August soon will be

a memory reality

forgot.

08/30/99.

That weeds

love hot, dry days

I haven't yet decided

is their blessing or their curse, but

they grow.

08/99.

You fell

a long, long way

from life to death and now,

frantic to get back, your burnt paws

would climb.

09/14/99.   "Electrocution of the Acrobat."

Broken

and ignored,

these trees with shattered arms

cry out to be remember'd in

their pain . . . .

09/17/99.

Because

winter's coming

pigeons and crows abound

strutting lawns like toughs, scaring off

sparrows.

09/26/99.

Eating

through a cricket,

grange ants gleam evil'y

in a noonday hour too full of

candor.

09/29/99.

Honking

importantly

geese fly high overhead

the white of their feathers flashing

like stars.

10/24/99.

Looking

everywhere

for a single great good

one finds many lesser goods so

tempting.

10/29/99.

Spatter

in evening sky

a flock of sparrows wheel

crazily and everything

revolves . . . .

11/99.

Lights out

and off to bed . . .

squirrels and birds turn in

but cat sits patient on the porch

and waits.

12/29/99.   "Night Life."

Sleeping

on a tree branch

one tired cardinal

could not stay awake to greet the

New Year.

12/31/99.

                    end of the third part of

                        A Book of Cinquains

Hung over,

white as a sheet,

the hesitant sun hangs

back behind the big broad shoulders

of clouds.

01/01/00.

Scourging

the land, winter

winds chase us all indoors;

on such a day futility's

made flesh.

01/14/00.

Falling

like a blizzard

a storm of light strikes him,

knocks the proud man from his high horse

to faith.

01/25/00.

Somewhat

in disarray,

these winter starlings peck

at piles of dirty snow chirping:

No luck!

01/29/00.

Four crows

feeding as one

then up and away 'til

the sky swallows them up—four crows

as one.

01/31/00.

How strange

to see a fly

born out of time buzzing

a snow bank—an explorer or

a fool?

02/05/00.

Darting,

flashing so fast

as to seem illusion

bluebird ruffles springtime's pimpled

branches.

03/24/00.

After

lady robin

swallows the landscape whole,

she limbers up her vocal chords

and sings!

04/11/00.   "Big Gulp."

Just when

I know you as

a grubbing rodent—Damn!—

if you don't leap through the air,

an angel.

04/23/00.   "Squirrel's Easter Leap."

Precise

operation—

thousands of maple seeds

descend on the wind conquering

with hope.

04/29/00.

Crown's lost,

Mac Donald's King

goes to bed without his

power—and so glory turns to

rubbish.

05/05/00.   "A Paper Crown Left on a Curb."

Big ants

roll like buses

'round small scurrying ones

like Godzilla's foot mine lands—damn

traffic!

05/06/00.   "A Busy Spring Day."

Stolen

by the maggot

your songs have become

stiff as your wings and lost in space

like you.

05/28/00.   "A Dead Songbird."

Swaying

too dizzily

crow launches itself, a kite

almost beaten back by the wind, caws

triumph.

05/29/00.

Poor bee

the big picture

eludes you—where I see

open window, you butt yourself

on glass.

05/30/00.

College

of cardinals

perched on a wire chirp

their disputations at bored

sparrows.

07/12/00.   "In Conclave."

Too late

to gain shelter,

this snail caught out of doors

fries in the sun, is eaten by

green flies.

07/18/00.   "On the Sunny Side of the Street."

I look

for what I know,

but less and less I see—

everything has changed while I

remain.

09/15/00.

Toy bear

sits on a lot

patiently waiting

a stranger's hand, a new place to

belong.

09/15/00.   "Giant Stuffed Panda—Cheap."

Bird cries

speckle the dawn,

there's a lot going on;

great journeys are afoot, plans are

hatching!

09/22/00.   "Here Comes Autumn!"

Surfeit

of rainfall makes

memories ping against

barriers of regret wet

with tears.

09/25/00.   "Pink Neon on Asbury Avenue."

Their lust

interrupted

by a speeding car, one

squirrel rushes on, the other

turns back . . . .

10/01/00.   "Fate-on-Wheels."

Waving

distractedly

the cricket on its back

signals the passerby he too

must die.

10/02/00.

Sawing

through nuts with teeth

is damned hard work yet

the squirrel with its nut seems so

peaceful . . .

10/04/00.

Gape-shot

by its beauty

I admire the dancer

black and speckled, storm-swept to

its death.

10/06/00.   "Poor Butterfly."

Shiny

in noon sunlight

ant's bobbing abdomen

makes its wavy way through the stone

courtyard.

10/14,15/00

Dancing

for my pleasure

over the hot coffee

smoke twists fantastically as

I smile.

11/21/00.   "Piping."

Clinging

to the pavement,

fallen leaves are shredded

by brooms—who'd have thought the dead so

stubborn?

11/24/00.   "Remember Me."

Static

makes second skin

as clothes bond to bodies

you strip them off and then you feel

flayed.

12/07/00.

end of the fourth part of

A Book of Cinquains

Screaming—

at God or me?—

the ragged man revolts

against the stream that carries him

away.

01/17/01.

Whole life

in a suitcase

go to look him up, he's

nowhere to be found—a minor

career.

01/19/01.   "Archive."

Snowy

sidewalks like a

blank page on which my feet

must write their destination when

I'm gone.

01/21/01.

Words blur,

refocus, blur—hands

forget to clasp the book

that falls with a thump—I'm up! I'm

tired.

01/26/01

New snow

too light to last

makes morning white and full

of promise—a whole day's worth of

beauty.

01/27/01.

Useless

the fear, therefore

like the squirrel running

along the wire, I too must run

on trust.

01/30/01.   "Spiritual Acrobatics."

Crowded

like a dance floor—

hands grabbing everywhere—

catch a pole or fall, damn lurching

trolley!

02/07/01.

Fallen

in flight it lies

shockingly outlined

against the pale concrete—a slate gray

feather.

02/10/01.

Dreaming

of spring, poor boy,

already bored by

pigeons and crows—where are those

robins?

02/14/01.

Turgid

winter river's

grayish yellow-green flow

waters barren bank's brush frozen

in death.

02/19/01.   "Brittle."

Tired

and in despair

poor cottonball of sun

tries to upstage a milk-glass sky

and fails.

02/22/01.   "Storm's Coming."

Scarce birds,

these cardinals,

and always rushing off

as if afraid to show their

beauty.

02/24/01.

Swiftly

as the wind blows

as a cardinal flies

my happiness gives way to slow

despair.

03/02/01.

Rolling

along the street

a little red balloon

passes me by, its business

urgent.

02/06/01.   "Commercial Traveler."

Behold—

sky full of stars

pearls against black velvet

or holes through which a greater light

shines forth?

02/10/01.

Whipping

across the park

it hits everywhere

at once—a bucket of cold water thrown—

this wind.

03/14/01.

Racing

ahead of me,

squirrel runs out of wall,

climbs tall tree to where I cannot

follow.

02/25/01.   "Game's Over."

How strange

that there should be

an unlucky number

for the luckiest day in all

our lives.

04/13/01.   "Good Friday."

Squabbles

of animals—

so unsightly to us—

they don't have our gift for smiling

treasons.

04/18/01.

Certain

of its powers

the robin prospects for

a worm that will not see the truth

and wait.

04/20/01.

Lovely

word "completed"—

it's a bit of freedom

nestled in the pocket of your

regard.

04/21/01.

First ant

of the season

cuts such a fine figure

posed on the concrete testing

the breeze.

04/24/01.

Squeezed

between your hands,

the clump of earth explodes—

do you then sense a setting off

of life?

05/12/01.

Touching

in their frailness,

and in their ugliness,

caterpillars dare cruel feet

to fall.

05/14/01.

Eyes on

turnip only,

Landseer's hare went to feed

the stoat, wherein lies an apt

moral.

05/18/01.

Curtain

of rainfall makes

this night unreal—a set

on which the dramas of the mind

unfold.

05/22/01.

Watching

a bird flying

through the rain reminds me

of the foolish virgins off to

buy oil.

05/26/01.   "Oil and Water."

Night walks

seem so dreamlike . . .

everything's washed out

under street lights, and each sound makes

you stare.

05/29/01.

Hopping

this way and that

robin accommodates

itself to an indifferent

tree stump.

06/05/01.

Lurid

in its redness

sun plummets like a stone

pink tinted azure drops splash in

my eyes.

06/20/01.

Gifting

master's front step

with a nice plump bird—dead—

the cat of the house justifies

itself.

06/24/01.   "The Sleep of the Just."

Thus heat

envelops you

and you begin to bake

'til the juice runs out your pores, then

you're done.

06/28/01.

Weeding

teaches us all

resignation; weeds don't

struggle against you, they know they'll

return.

06/30/01.   "Weeding—II."

Torching

Popsicle Co.

another bit of old

Philly goes to warm the hands of

its ghosts.

07/02/01.

Flinging

my old sandal—

a desperation play—

I crush the roach caught scurrying

from view.

07/21/01.

Like fields

across the sky

upon which a pilgrim

could walk all the way to Heaven . . .

these clouds.

07/22/01.

Runs down

like a curtain,

heat of a summer day,

while you caught in its folds flail for

an out.

07/25/01.

How nice

to feel the sleep

come creeping upon you—

everything's relaxed and you

let go.

07/29/01.

Dreaming

ancient days,

did he once dare surmise

what stretch'd beneath the waves he knew

so well?

07/31/01.   "The Poet Cavafy Visits
                           Cleopatra's Palace."

Swooping

in the sunlight

pigeons duel with

sparrows for the crumbs and a dog leaps

for joy.

08/02/01.

The Past

holds many truths

sometimes like nesting dolls,

sometimes like glass chips in a vast

design.

08/03/01.

Heat too

transfigures You,

turns sun-like in mind's eye,

'til we tremble, feeling the flames

of Hell!

08/06/01.   "Fundamentalist's Transfiguration."

Sadness

of locked doors—

each one a chance wasted,

or else an opportunity

withheld.

08/11/01.

Hobbling

its zigzag path

to nowhere, this housefly,

gold armor disarray'd, pumps its

torn wing.

08/16/01.   "Patroclus."

Flipped

onto its back,

divine cicada finds

the world a different, treeless

wasteland.

Beating

its legs in vain,

what can it do but stay

for a shoe or the ants to end

the wait?

08/25/01. "The Fall."

Enough!

You're dead, fool bug,

you can't undo the thing

or gain reprieve because a leg's

waving . . . .

09/05/01.

Begging

a squirrel stands

but man, gifted with pride,

makes himself small, the better to

feign worth.

09/08/01.

Dried,

trod underfoot,

even dog dime changes,

looks dead . . . no longer bursting with

shit-ness.

09/15/01.

How soon

it all ended!—

the cicadas' singing

almost before I noticed

their song.

09/16/01.

If I

indifferent

let the parade pass by,

then who can save me from my choice

of deaths?

09/21/01.

Saddest

of rains—leafstorm

whose falling shakes my soul

into brief awareness of time's

regime.

10/02/01.   "An Apolitical."

Tasting . . .

imagining . . .

one rebukes the other

when possibilities boil down

to one.

10/09/01.

Gulping

its share of crumbs

the sparrow does not ask

will there be more nor think how much

to save.

10/10/01.

In time

It all happens,

The oranges and reds

seep into the sea of green then

change it.

10/14/01.

Showy

hates the subtle

and shouts banish whispers—

do opposites attract just to

destroy?

10/19/01.

Envy

propels the will

to have—and passions goad

the weak man 'til he chokes himself

on gain!

10/20/01.

Painful

makes you aware

of painless which before

you would have defined as mere

absence.

09/25/01.

Ponder

the myriad

intricacies of fate—

pretend it's wisdom but believe

it's luck.

09/26/01.

So long

I have known you

that your mysteries

have become my jewels, lovely

stranger.

09/27/01.   "To S—Belatedly."

It runs—

in spite of all—

no deals, no prayers stop

the fated ticking rhythm of

life's clock.

11/01/01.

Good, bad;

bad for squirrel

crushed on the roadway,

good for crow who wins out over

hunger.

11/08/01.   "The Fair Winds Blows . . ."

Treetop

perching squirrel

plays at being a crow,

but lacking authority acts

the clown.

11/16/01.   "In Borrowed Robes."

Wishful

thinking—prayer

of the unbeliever

that everything will turn out right

despite . . . .

11/19/01.

Cold out—

trees nearly nude

quaver in the twilight

and those homeward-bound footsteps fall

faster.

11/20/01.

Undone

at the day's end

many things worth doing

whose phantoms will ring doorbells in

your dreams.

11/24/01.

Swarming

purposefully

over a mint jelly

ants claim their prize before they know

its worth.

11/25/01.   "'Taint what you do..."

Some days

You just can't win

although you always try

and end up feeling foolish but

alive.

11/26/01.

Moist night,

a great big womb

giving birth to nothing . . .

walking around in it I feel

empty.

11/29/01.

Andrew,

rational man,

draws lines around his Lord

by questioning the aptness of

the means.

11/30/01.   "Feast of St. Andrew—II."

Darkness

of winter night,

so purgatorial,

promises nothing other than

the dawn.

12/04/01.

Hellscreen—

cockroach trapped

in shiny white bathtub,

all that smooth porcelain—nowhere

to hide.

12/07/01.

Hiding

in a cypress

squirrel reveals itself

because it can't stay quiet—like

some men.

12/08/01.

Cloud banks

like fresh bruises

underscore misery

of houses beat down by sky that's

too vast.

12/15/01.

Doing's

a restless child

who makes poor parent Thought

go gray overnight with such bold

actions.

12/17/01.

Insult

to the darkness,

a final band of light

rallies on the horizon, sings

of day . . . .

12/18/01.

Weary

of ceaseless toil,

the cog in the machine

pauses mid-rotation, asking:

Wherefore?

12/21/01.   "Broken."

Restless

as in Nature

where stoppage is decline,

I dream of one eternal calm

Moment.

12/31/01.

The end of

A Book of Cinquains